Scenes from Fylde Coast and Country

Memories of

Warton, Bryning, Ballam, Westby,

Lytham St. Annes, Marton Moss,

and Little Marton

by

Kathleen Eyre

The Lancashire Library

1985

FOREWORD

In recent years there has been a steady growth in the publication of illustrated local history books. The more confined the area the more detailed the study. No one has contributed more to the study of the Fylde – the original Fylde – than Kathleen Eyre.

Kathleen Eyre's most valuable contribution to the study of local history has been her technique in gathering information, and the towns and villages of the Fylde have been her gathering grounds. She sought out the oldest inhabitants and painstakingly took down their accounts in their own words. From these she described life in the native thatched three-bay cottage. Memory is fallible and favours things pleasant. If she erred at all it was on the side of optimism, but she hit the mark when she described the effects of poverty and the eternal hard grind. When the visit of the itinerant pack-man becomes a red letter day, the isolation of the villages can be felt.

However, much has changed, and it is valuable to have, in words and pictures, such a readable reminder of life in the Fylde.

P. P. Hall
Chairman of the Library and Leisure Committee
1981–1985

Cover illustration: *Sketch by T. A. Clarke.*

Published by Lancashire County Council Library and Leisure Commitee

1985

ISBN 0 902228 56 0

Printed by John Bentley (Printers) Ltd.
A member of the Dunn & Wilson Group

Acknowledgments

During the preparation of this publication, the author has received help and co-operation from many sources, for which she will ever be sincerely grateful.

First and foremost, she would like to record her indebtedness and appreciation to the following – to a friend and former colleague, Mr. W. E. "Ted" Gray, who devoted much time to the preparation of photographic prints, often from faded originals; to Stanley Brown for his scraperboard of Lytham Beach, for prints of boatyard, railway station and Vicarage, and for his unfailing encouragement and assistance; to Frank Dean, long-time friend and collaborator, for the tram pictures and for several of his photographs from Heyhouses, the West End and Marton Moss in the 1960's; to Tommy and Anne Dowbiggin for loan of 2 photographs from Division Lane and 1 from Warton; to John Green for his pen-sketch of the lighthouse cottages, St. Annes; to their President, Roy Hargreaves, and members of Warton Historical Society for six village street scenes; to her late and most dear friend, Jean Hanson, a few of whose photographs have been reproduced in memory of their shared interest in Local History; to all who in times gone by have allowed their precious recollections to be placed on record for the benefit of posterity; and to the publishers, Lancashire County Library and, in particular Mrs. M. Sheridan, who have made it possible for this collection to be made available to the public.

From half a lifetime's comprehensive collection, the whole of which will eventually be passed to the Lancashire County Records Office, it was difficult to limit the material to fit into the available space. The area chosen, therefore, begins at Warton and travels coastwards to Squires Gate, including Lytham St. Annes and touching lightly upon the rural hinterland including Bryning-with-Kellamergh, Ballam and Westby, Commonside, Ansdell, Heyhouses, the West End of old Lytham Manor (north St. Annes), Cross Slack, Division Lane and Mad Nook to Chapel Road, Marton Moss, Squires Gate and Little Marton.

As her criteria, the author has chosen those scenes which have entirely vanished; have changed beyond recognition; or very shortly are expected to be swept into oblivion. That which can still be visited and seen as it was, has not been included, the whole idea being to evoke memories, to keep the past alive, to remind young and old and the generations still to come, how the Fylde folk fared in coastal and country communities in those far off days before the internal combustion engine brought in a new era and obliterated an honourable heritage and a whole way of life.

"Kate's Pad",
Lime Grove,
ST. ANNES, LYTHAM ST. ANNES.

KATHLEEN EYRE.

WARTON'S 18TH CENTURY PEG AND POST WINDMILL c. 1900, complete with weather-cock. It had common sails, i.e., not louvred, and canvas sail-cloths had to be attached at different angles, as required, either at "sword-point", "dagger-point" or "full sail". A post-mill is clearly marked on Wm. Yates' Map (1786) and a few years later Thomas Strickland, husbandman, and John Strickland, miller, of Warton and Ballam, secured a lease in 1790. The latter remained until 1843 when he offered "the mill and kiln" to the Clifton Agent, as "I am now getting old and no-one to manage the same for me". Before the end of that year he was apologising for the rent having fallen into arrears and would have "come over to Lytham" himself but was unable "on account of old age".

Warton, an Anglian long-street village metamorphosed by the aircraft industry, still had an ancient look in the 1920's. Its green gaps, homely cottages, a hint of thatch and an almost Sabbath quiet, belied its former importance as the weard-ton or watch-town guarding the busy crossing over the Ribble estuary.

Resolute travellers along Magnum Stratum, the high road from Chester to the north, crossed the Mersey, proceeded overland to the Ribble and the foot-track at low tide from Hesketh Bank to Warton, and thence through the Fylde and Over-Wyre to Lancaster and via Morecambe Bay to Grange, Furness and Scotland. The perils and discomforts were legion. Casualty figures were not confined to strangers passing through.

At the time of Domesday Survey (1086), "Wartun" had four carucates, or 4 x 120 acres, under cultivation, showing progress since the arrival of the Angles c. 700 A.D. The Singletons were prominent here during the Middle Ages though, a hundred years ago, Col. John Talbot Clifton, Squire of Lytham, was the most extensive landowner.

Jolly Thomas Tyldesley of Fox Hall, Blackpool, whose diary gives us fascinating glimpses of fashionable life along the coast between 1712–1714, describes a typical May outing. "About eight in ye morning went over Ribble to Ormskirke race", he wrote having galloped, accompanied by his man, to Warton where the guide would ensure a safe crossing. (There were less convenient routes via Walton-le-Dale bridge or Penwortham ford).

During the 17th century, the "Guide over the River" usually charged 6d. per single crossing. The traveller intending to return, as did Tyldesley after hobnobbing at Ormskirk with "a great company off the best in ye county", would fix a convenient hour to be met. In the Lancashire County Records (QSP/118/7) William Tomlinson petitioned the "Sessions of Peace holden at Preston" on 4th October 1655 pleading that he had "served the people ... for the space of ffortie yeares and upward and hath been readie upon all seasonable tymes and occasions with himself and his horse to guide and preserve passengers from the danger of the water" ... having in the process "lost about the number of ten horses to his great dammage and impoverishment" though willing to continue. To the request for a grant towards "the buyinge of a horse fitt for that service as in your wisdomes may seem meete", the Justices responded with a laconic "Nul", meaning nothing granted, and Tomlinson presumably bought his own nag or retired from the service. Ten lost horses in forty years confirms the dangers besetting even the experts. Many an unwary pedestrian was overtaken by the tide and washed up on the river-bank and early this century corpses were laid "waiting upon the Coroner" in a derelict cottage near the water.

On Yates' map, 1786, two properties appear, each called "Guides House". One, obviously, was the Inn. Its records go back to 1656 when James Bonney "an honest poore labouringe man" of the village whom 31 honest Wartonians considered "verie fitting to keepe an Alehowse, he beinge very able to give intertaynement and lodginge both to man and horse" applied to Quarter Sessions for a licence. He was well behaved, had never "kept or harbored any lewd or idle companie in his howse" and there was a great want "of a sufficient Inne". Warton had once boasted "three or fower Alehowses in itt, and now noe but one and that not able to give intertaynment to all that travell that way". In this case, on 7th October 1656 (QSP/134/3), the application was "Allowed". After many years, the

WARTON PEG AND POST MILL — all that remains now, standing on spare land up Mill Lane.

cottage inn was replaced by a commodious whitewashed pub with its own landing stage. It was a landmark, visible from Lytham, attracting the yachting and fishing fraternities and ramblers, bicyclists and excursionists by the hundred. On a good Sunday afternoon when there were 240 old pennies to the pound, as many as 30 wagonnettes or chars-a-bancs would roll up and 2d. cups of tea would bring in as much as £7.0s.0d. The Inn premises could not cope and a large wooden cafe was built, along with one or two holiday bungalows let for the season. At the river's edge, resembling miniature Noah's arks, were houseboats that could be rented by the week. Except for one, they were smashed up during the great inundation of the sea which battered the Fylde coast in 1927.

Guides House, in the old days, was popular with inlanders from Preston and further afield. The Blackburn folk, being good spenders, were particularly welcome. Twenty years ago, the late William Fenton (85), a Wartonian-born, recalled "as nice a night as I ever hed" down at the Guides one Sunday evening in August. "I was wed at the time and me and a pal went and sat in the front rowm". It was pretty quiet until a chara or two arrived and a boatload or two "who came down the river from Lytham". Then the fun started. "Front rowm geet full, a young woman got on th'piano and a big hefty lass from a boat-house ged agate singing, and By! Could she SING! Tom Singleton, ex-police Inspector, hed it then. I went to schoo' wi' him. We hed many a good sing-song theer!" Did any fights break out? Apparently, "the wife's uncle" talked about the days when the banks were built along the marshes. "Gangs of English and Irish navvies went to the Ship Inn at Freckleton and there was blood running down the street, there was that much fighting. I know her uncle was busy among it . . . but at Guides! . . . I never see any".

WARTON – The Guides House Hotel

WARTON – The Bungalow Guides House

WARTON – The Cafe, Guides House

WARTON – Guides Lodge

WARTON – Houseboats on Riverbank

"OLD JACKIE HIGHAM'S PLACE" on the riverbank, Warton, near Guides House, from a watercolour painted in 1906.

Records paint a different picture. Warton's Parson George Wylie protested to Squire Clifton's Agent about licensing hours being ignored and customers brawling, particularly on Sundays. The constable who had endeavoured to clear the premises at the proper hour had been set upon by "some of the individuals present". The parson was nervous of open meddling for fear that his wayward flock would stay away from church altogether, becoming "tenfold greater blackguards than before". He dreaded even more the strapping gangers employed in building the training walls off Warton for the Ribble Navigation Company. Flouting orders to the contrary, the scallywags persisted in digging out clay and gravel for filling purposes from Squire Clifton's foreshore causing £20's-worth of damage, imperilling the route over the Ribble and depriving the official guide of making a living. It took years to complete the massive scheme to control the capricious Ribble up to the dock at Preston. By then, after only four years, Parson Wylie had resigned the Warton living in 1844.

Guides House became as respectable a licensed house as could be found anywhere in the kingdom. Early this century, a child grew up there when her Grandfather Richardson, a retired Master Mariner, was landlord. In 1906 she persuaded a Freckleton artist to put something in her autograph album and he sketched "Owd Jackie Higham's place" which was possibly the original Guide's House. Frances Bonney, the inn servant who may have been descended from the original licensee, nipped over daily to rip out loose timbers for kindling. There were memories of practising at the piano by the light of an oil lamp; of sudden squalls and punts overturning; of bodies being washed up and, once, of seven corpses lying stiff and silent in an outbuilding; of her father, a Stockbroker at Southport who rowed across on Mondays and returned on Fridays having a heart-stopping

PRIMROSE HILL COTTAGE, BANK LANE, condemned in 1960 and rescued and restored in the nick of time by Mr. and Mrs. C. E. Harris, who turned it into a bungalow, was "lately erected on Warton Mill Hill" in 1777 and leased upon payment of £5.5s.0d., and a yearly rent of 1s.0d., to widow Rachel Watson (38) and her two young sons, formerly of Treales. By 1838 the rent had risen to "£6.. for the present" payable to the Clifton Estate. The old thatch, reduced to powder, was still there under the metal sheeting in 1960 when several blocked up windows were discovered, probably due to Window Tax. The little boy in the photograph is now a venerable Wartonian, Mr. W. Bickerstaffe.

ST. PAUL'S CHURCH, WARTON, consecrated 1725, rebuilt in last quarter of the 19th century.

TOWNSEND'S, the blacksmith's and wheelwright's, on site of Smithy Garage.

experience on the marsh as he made for his boat moored at Hesketh Bank. It was harvest time. Thousands of rats had congregated in the moonlight, a vast menacing army as far as the eye could see. Fortunately, they were bloated with overfeeding. Mr. Glover kept his nerve, strode along purposefully, climbed into his boat and struck off across the river. The same resolute gentleman caused a German spy to be nabbed during the first world war. The stranger had been spotted near Guides House making sketch maps of the Ribble estuary. Afterwards, he engaged a local salmon fisherman to row him across to Southport where he was arrested by the police and identified as a German agent.

Guides House was obliterated in the 1940's as effectively as if it had been bombed from the air. Where British Aerospace operates, there was already an R.A.F. airfield when the Americans arrived with larger aircraft needing longer runways. The Air Ministry, therefore, ordered the inn along with eight or ten ancient farms, several residences built by retired sea captains and some of the finest agricultural land in the north-west to be sacrificed to the demands of war. Heartbreak, hardship and resentment lingered on for decades after the Yanks departed never, some said, having used the new runways which faced the wrong direction in the first place.

View up the village street early this century.

Village street looking west.

Jollifications outside the Clifton Arms Inn, now Pickwick Tavern, pre first world war.

Fewer there are now who can recall that world apart, that community of old and new dwellings overlooking the river, with figureheads from old sailing ships decorating tiny cottage gardens and families too shy to open the door more than two inches to a neighbour and never to a stranger; of great snow-ups and three fields to plod over to collect the daily papers; and pilots waving from the river and cargo vessels sailing at close quarters up to Preston.

In 1932 a celebrated artist, the late T. A. Clarke of St. Annes, sat happily sketching on Warton bank. His delightful study appears on the front cover. It lay forgotten for years before he passed it into my keeping with permission to reproduce it. It set me off tracking down the story of the "Old Manor House", fortunately in the lifetime of Mrs. Alice Singleton of the Nook Farm, then a youthful octogenarian with scarcely a grey hair and a bubbling sense of humour. She had been born c. 1883 at lonely Penketh Farm along the river-bank only a field's width from the steep drop down to the water, one of many children, nine of whom survived, never ailing a thing nor seeing a doctor except for accidents.

"We weren't brought up like precious china", she chuckled, remembering how they often slipped, fell into the water, dried their clothes on a fence and told no-one. "But we were always hard up", she added as, indeed, everybody was when wages were 7s.0d. or 8s.0d. a week for farm workers. Women never summoned the doctor for confinements but "did" for each other when the time came.

The occasional visits of Uncle Will Archer were an excitement. "Sailing mad" from boyhood, he ran off to sea and stayed "foreign sailing" for years on end. His colourful tales from far-off places kept the household wide-eyed for hours on end. Mariners were as hard up as farm workers in those days, so they didn't look for presents; his company and his stories were pleasure enough. Besides, toys were rarities. "We had none, but we had FUN".

Pupils paid 2d. a week to attend Warton School but young Alice broke her arm at eleven and never went back. When the family moved to Freckleton, she "worked at the Mill at the looms". Later, they went to Ballam, then to Peel from where she married "the best husband in all the world". They started school together on the same day, learned their tables and ABC's together. He died 6 years before our meeting in 1964.

After marriage, they lived in Bank Lane for twelve months but, because "I was the farmer in the family, we took this cottage for 3s.1d. a week, paid half-yearly, to have a bit of land to farm; and after six years we bought our own farmhouse at Warton Lodge". (That speaks volumes for the hard work and sacrifice that went on!). Mr. Singleton only earned 14/- a week with 1d. "stopped for the hospital", at Lytham Shipyard. He walked to work along a path one foot wide beside a sheer drop down to the water. Fortunately, despite mists, he never fell in; nor did his faithful wife who rose early to get him off to work at five in the morning.

Studying the sketch, she murmured: "I did love this old house of happiness. There was neither rat nor mouse, nor cockroach; it was a real healthy house". From left to right, the accommodation was identified beginning with the "chamber", then the "house-part" or living room with a hearth and a great canopy firehood supported by a sturdy beam. "You had to bend to get under it, but then you could straighten up. You were soon reminded if you forgot to duck!" Chairs could even be placed by the fire under the canopy. The central portion, slated and added to the original thatched cruck cottage, had a kitchen workroom and a tiny staircase to the sleeping area under the roof. Next came the shippon "where I kept pigs, breeding sows, never cows", said Mrs. Singleton whose first three children were born at the Old Manor House, one on a bitterly cold January day when even the milk froze in the jug. On such occasions an old aunt called in but, with toddlers also to care for, "I never was in bed, but I never told!", she recalled, adding: "Necessity is a hard taskmaster. You had to learn to contrive".

The Fylde Folk of 100 years ago were an heroic breed who had never heard of "essential services". "We caught rainwater in the old butt for household use and carried drinking water across two fields from Gardiner's (later Archers' Farm). I hadn't an idle minute . . . always along the shore picking up coals" (spilt from barges from the Wigan coalfields heading for Lytham and St. Annes on Sea). "I baked all my own bread – there was no money to buy a loaf – made cheese, grew vegs and fruit, produced eggs and butter". One time, the old sow shot the bolt from the outside and locked her in the pig place. "I kept shouting and our little Jack, who was still in frocks, toddled across and let me out – or I might have been there yet!", she laughed. "We were hard up but happy. Often, if I ate, there was nothing for him. I've gone hungry many a time and told no-one". Her good man had only one indulgence in life – his half-ounce of twist 'bacca. He even gave that up once saying "we'll be penniless", but she still put it on the list for Harry Sallows who brought the groceries from Lytham every week. "I used to tell him it wasn't worth coming for my bit, but he kept coming".

Six happy years and three kiddies after moving in, the Singletons had saved enough to buy a place of their own at Warton Lodge. It wasn't too difficult to leave this charming old place. "There was no other house near and no-one to talk to, and I thought the kids were going gormless!", laughed the former tenant. After 14 years at Warton Lodge they bought Nook Farm, Warton, where they prospered and were supremely content . . . until war broke out and the Air Ministry moved in and with only a fortnight's notice everything but the farmhouse was flattened by the bulldozers. Mrs. Singleton lived on in the farmhouse until 1967 when, at the age of 84, she was reunited with her life's love whom she first met in the 1880's.

Approaching Warton from Lytham, West End Lane dives sharply off to the left and wanders through a belt of quietness and gently swelling green. Too bad, if you missed it when the bonny cruck cotages were still there, squatting at the laneside. Typical Fylde homesteads, three centuries old, they were built on timber supports with walls of clay and sea cobbles. Their old thatch had disappeared under protective sheeting. The bother of replenishing no longer appealed to a modern generation.

In 1964, in the last white cottage amid a garden rioting with colour, dwelt old John Hogarth, at 85 "th'owdest-born fella i' Warton", a dozen years after his thatch disappeared. He had only lived in two houses in all his long life, having been born in a low thatched cottage "six storey lung and one heygh" next to the old Clifton Arms in the village. It was two cots knocked into one, with clay floors and timber crucks. From there, at 24 with 2s.0d. a week spending money and £13 in the bank, he married Emmeline Hankinson, fellow Wartonian, and moved into that cosy place at the West End. His bride worked at Freckleton mill starting at 6 a.m., and as he also had to be off at an ungodly hour, they only saw their home in daylight for months on end on Sundays.

On a modest income, they kept everything in apple-pie order, grew their own produce, tended the hens. "I've had me knuckles i' everybody's business except plumbing but never served my time to nowt", chuckled John. "Many lads were bund 'prentice in them days but

WARTON, WEST END LANE. John Hogarth standing at the door of his "crutch" cottage which was always warm, cosy and beautifully maintained, in the early 1960's. A modern bungalow occupies the site now.

WARTON, WEST END LANE . . . looking back up the lane towards the Lytham road junction, with Mr. John Hogarth's thatched cottage (extreme left) and its companions before the modern builder arrived.

WARTON, WEST END LANE — one of the low clay and cruck cottages, originally thatched, which remained occupied until three or four years ago when the site was cleared to make way for modern properties. The small dormer window was at floor level in the tiny sleeping chambers in the roof space. The downstairs windows had been greatly enlarged.

WARTON — the notice above the door (left) reads: Townsends, Grocers. The property has since become the village grocers and Post Office. This is how it looked almost 80 years ago.

if they broke (opted out) they got jailed!" Holidays were unknown to the couple. "I always walked to Lytham Club Day and Freckleton, too, if we could afford it afterwards." He left school at 13, worked at Freckleton brickcroft "carrying off" from 7 a.m. till 8 p.m., six days a week with only minutes snatched to eat breakfast, dinner and tea, for 10s.0d. a week. Sickened after a few months, he transferred to another brick-croft in Hornby Road, Blackpool for 10s.0d. a week plus bonus "but they never give us no bonus!" It meant trudging to Lytham Station every Monday morning with a basket containing all his food except bread, returning at weekend. So, after paying for his bed, "How much did me mother make out of me, eh?", he wondered. That didn't last long either and at 16 he went to Windy Harbour Farm, Warton, and for three long years received 6s.0d. a week and his food. A qualified cowman got £18 p.a., and an experienced horseman £25 p.a., in those days, master and men working every hour of daylight, long before paid overtime was thought of. But, as a married man, there was precious little to fritter away from his 18s.0d. a week, with 1d. stopped for the hospital, for ten years working as horse driver for the Lytham Shipbuilding Company, starting at 6 a.m. There was no public transport. A chap called Crowther from Freckleton Naze even had to be there early enough to get up steam to blow the horn at 5.55 a.m., for no extra pay.

In John's young days, the old thatched Clifton Arms had two bowling greens at the rear and "they used to come theer frae Kirkham and Lytham and fight", he remembered. There, on his fortnightly rounds, Owd Duffy the Packman once rested his bundles and dawdled over a double whisky. The old cock-sod was still discernible, a circular depression in a field east of the highway, where locals enjoyed many a bloodthirsty meeting.

John's father, a fisherman, landed his catches at Lytham's mud dock with neither horse nor pony to help him. One stormy night, he called for his pal who declined to set out saying: "Nay, id's a bit too rough for me". So father faced it alone, hauled in a mighty catch, "filled the buttery floor with salmon" which sold so well at Preston that he bought a pony. When he could afford a trap he went into the haulage business. "He'd cart anyone to Preston and back and wait as lung as you like, for 6s.0d." said John, recalling extra carting for the local wheelwright, like bringing turf from the Moss and tubs of water to cool the wheels. "Later, he got a trap with a hood over for carrying passengers". On one famous occasion, when there was a circus on at Lytham, he counted 22, big and little, emerging from the single-horse two-wheeler trap! "We put forms on a spring cart and took folks to Blackpool and on Whit Mondays we used old coal carts, polished the horses' hooves and carried parties from Blackpool to Preston".

Country living was plain but wholesome. "Flukes sold for a few coppers a score. We had 'em strung on a line at th'back o'th'house and we'd poo 'em off, throw 'em on t'fire and ayt 'em. We were browt up on noddin' puddin', throdkins an' curran' cake. Ay've etten monny a ton o'curran's an' sheyp-heyd an pluck", smiled John who could remember 12-week frosts and skating on the frozen brook all the way from Kirkham to Brook Bridge Cottage, Warton (west of the highway) where an old couple, to quote a quaint expression, were "living clumsy". As a lad, he spent many a mischievous hour with his catapult "batting away at th'owd cock", the weathervane a-top Warton windmill. "Trotting Johnny" pounded through from Preston collecting rags in "gurt big seed secks", hurrying back in the evenings like an elf with a huge balloon on its shoulder, silhouetted against the evening sky. "Owd Dick Ashton", the cockler, passed through regularly with his wife "frae Kirkham, allus wet through an' shiverin'". One time, she came alone. "He's getten his leg in a tight stockin' an' he's hev a job ta ged id out!", she called, indicating that "Owd Dick" had landed up in jail.

WARTON – Mr. and Mrs. Bickerstaffe of Further Hillock Farm, c. 1920, with their very smart turn-out.

"BRYNING, "HILL COTTAGE", BRYNING HILL, where the author spent scores of happy Saturday afternoons visiting Miss Annie Dugdale, retired Infants' Mistress of Warton School, and her ever proliferating family of puss-cats. (At one famous count, there were nineteen, in addition to the pet dog Pat, which died in 1964). Miss Dugdale loved reminiscing; remembered the first John Bull bus that ran from Preston to Lytham, and the tarpaulin-covered wagonettes that plied before that; recalled "Trotting Johnny" Bradshaw rising to the dignity of a donkey cart, offering lifts on it and handing out donkey stones for rags. Electricity was only installed in the 1940's. It was oil lamps before that, relying on the visits of "Paraffin Joe" Rawstrone and later his son "Paraffin Jack". "I have bobbins yet that Mother bought off the old basketwomen", she told me, having been born and having spent all her days in this genuine old cruck cottage with the rough outlines of tree branches clearly visible in the two inter-connecting bedrooms under the roof.

BRYNING, "CRIMBLE COTTAGE" pictured in the early 1960's, has since been demolished and the site, at the foot of Bryning Hill on the road to Wrea Green, remains vacant to this day. The old thatch had been covered with sheeting. Otherwise, the cottage almost retained its original appearance and seemed sturdy and certainly picturesque enough to be preserved for ever.

KELLAMERGH – a country group 100 years ago.

Pampering was unknown. Men would walk to St. Annes and beyond to find work. Few possessed one of the old solid-tyre bicycles and once, when two bright sparks set off to pedal to Southport, the whole village turned out, waved them off and watched out for their safe return. From Old John, who produced the worm-eaten remains of his old wooden rake, I received my only lesson in thatching. "Tha wants a ton o' wheat straya (straw). Keep it wet, blacker the better, while a goose sits (31 days) and ya mun be very particler wi' each section. Comb id out an' give id a good batting wi't'back o' your rake. Mind you", he warned, "birds used to play Hamlet wi' id and id hed ta be done every five or six year, besides patchin'!" No wonder the old tradition had lost its appeal, though Old John kept it up until into his seventies. And even a decade later, after a hard day's work, "batching" for himself and tending 200 hens, he would leap on his bike and pedal off to Lytham for a hard game of bowls.

We don't seem to make them like that any more!

Susanna Preston's father, James Preston, a railway worker who transferred from Faringdon, Preston, to Wrea Green in the early 1880's and rose to the position of Stationmaster there, moving later to Thornton. In the year following the death of Susanna's mother, he married a young wife and produced a second family. He, his two wives and a couple of daughters are buried in the same grave at Wrea Green.

BALLAM SCHOOLHOUSE and the beautiful and talented Miss Susanna Preston, Schoolmistress in the 1890's, universal favourite of the young and old of the district and a splendid organiser of field days, concerts, fund raising efforts and diversions of all kinds. She resigned at Easter 1911 to marry a Lytham widower, Walter Gledhill (46), father of three teenage children, who transported her across the Ribble, first to Hesketh Bank and later to Southport where she survived into her 97th year.

BALLAM SCHOOL GROUP with the more mature Miss Preston (right) and her able lieutenant, Miss Banks (left) early this century.

TOM PRESTON, the handsome son of the Wrea Green Station-master, who bore an uncanny resemblance to his sister Susanna. After a broken romance with a girl from Stanah, he cleared off to Canada and never returned though he corresponded for many years with Miss Preston (later Mrs. Gledhill).

Ballam, a mile or two inland, where green fields gently rise and dip near the eastern boundary of Lytham Manor, was named by the Angles from the O.E. ham, signifying a homestead, and ball, or mound marking a boundary. Even today Ballam is an obscure place, less than a village, hardly a hamlet. This is farming territory. Flat fields spread towards Moss Side and on the left of the road leading to Lower Ballam and Westby a gentle hillock or two break the monotony.

Originally folks settled here well clear of the waterlogged mosslands before the great reclamation. Until the early 1950's one or two old whitewashed and thatched cottages still survived. All have been destroyed, modernised beyond recognition, or replaced – as, for instance, the lodgekeeper's cottage at the extremity of Squire Clifton's park. Bridge Hall Farm (1766) opposite is greatly enlarged since the Whitesides arrived shortly after Queen Victoria's Golden Jubilee in 1887. After losing their mother and two sisters, the three bachelor brothers Whiteside, devout Catholics all, stayed on until they were borne in turn to Saltcotes Cemetery before the first world war.

At the junction of the lane leading to Northhouses stands the red brick school house built in 1890, four years before her death, at the instigation of Lady Eleanor Cecily Clifton whose initials appear on the frontage. Her haughty demeanour – she was descended from the Lowthers – belied her warmth of heart and a genuine concern for the tenants whose homes and schoolrooms she was pleased to visit. Sixty years after her death they were still recalling her sayings and doings in awe and admiration.

In the early days of the school, Miss Susanna Preston (1874–1971) daughter of the Stationmaster at Wrea Green, former pupil and later pupil teacher at the school there, was

BALLAM – rethatching the two cottages which stood opposite the school, c. 1910, with a helping hand from Mrs. Grace Sowerbutts, the cowman's wife, and her two boys. The youth on the ladder was Mr. Edward Swann who died just short of his 94th birthday in December 1983. The bearded thatcher was the expert, Mr. Nicholas Gillett, of "Willow Cottage", Westby. The white building in the background was Bridge Hall Farm (now pebble-dashed and greatly extended).

THE ORIGINAL WHITE FARM-HOUSE, LOWER BALLAM, dated 1701, as it appeared up to the early 1920's. The alterations and additions are clearly visible upon closer inspection.

"WILLOW COTTAGE", WESTBY, well set back from the Ballam Road to Wrea Green has lately been extended and re-roofed with Norfolk reeds. This is how it looked in the 1960's when the author called upon Mr. Jem Gillett (76) who still re-thatched with genuine wheatstraw. He was the son of a famous Fylde thatcher, "Owd Nicky" Gillett who survived to the age of 85, and grandson of another expert thatcher, Jem Gillett who suddenly took up farming at Newton at 79 and whose life was tragically cut short at 82 when "he geet lommerted in some bailing wire and tummelled an' wur never reet after that". The accommodation (left), also once thatched, was the labourer's cottage, and there was once a twin to it on the right hand side. There were pitchpine beams, with slots and hooks and nails on which to hang a variety of domestic paraphernalia; and a curving flight of stairs to the bedrooms was hidden behind a door with a sneck latch. Jem's father, "Owd Nicky", could call to mind a handloom weavers' shed where a number of weavers worked before the Kirkham mills put them out of business. It was in the field opposite during his childhood but the floor was still to be found, just below the topsoil.

appointed Mistress at Ballam. She was beautiful and talented, a proficient pianist and organist and a splendid organiser of treats and concerts which greatly delighted both young and old of the district. Assisted first by Miss Earl and later by Miss Banks, a most loyal lieutenant, she ran an excellent educational establishment which had to be extended in 1910 at a cost of £337. The project was closely supervised by a Clifton Estate employee, Mr. Walter Gledhill (46) of Lytham, a widower and father of three teenage offspring. Miss Preston was in her mid-thirties. They fell in love. Miss Preston resigned at Easter 1911 and local farmers subscribed 30 golden sovereigns towards her leaving gift. The school operated until 1978, peaking at 35 pupils but averaging 25 and falling below 20 when closure was expected. The building is still used for Church of England Services organised from Wrea Green, and for various local meetings.

The identity of the bonny thatched farmhouse at "Lower Ballam" puzzled the writer (who inherited a collection of old glass slides) for many years until the mystery was solved recently by a chance visit to White House Farm. It is cradled in a green bowl, sheltered from the biting east winds by a considerable hummock, and set well back enough from the road to accord it all the privacy its ancient heart could desire. The thatch has gone. Windows have had "the treatment". There are bits added and doorways blocked that appear in the photograph of about 1924. This was always a house of some considerable substance, with solid walls up to 18″ thick, of mixed bonding Old English hand-made bricks. Two original windows, one down, and the old chimney stacks have survived. So have the inglenook with a huge oak beam across the hearth and a 17th century-type

panelled door leading into a small spice room. There are relics of old hooks in ancient oak beams but only one staircase, where there were two. Indeed, for a spell, the property was converted into two cottages. Now it is one very attractive modernised home with the original date, 1701, carved into the wooden door lintel leading into the porch and the initials RE ^K AK signifying occupation by man and son. It was the original homestead of White House Farm set upon a rise along Ballam Road leading towards Westby and looks set to stand for several centuries more.

LYTHAM, East Beach, showing St. John's Church (1849), Windmill (1805), old Lifeboat House (1851). (Scraperboard study by Stanley Brown)

Lytham St. Annes

On 31st March 1922, by Charter of Incorporation, Lytham and St. Annes on the Sea became a Municipal Borough, an event celebrated on Charter Day, 1st May 1922. (Lytham St. Annes became part of Fylde Borough in 1974).

Lytham, an ancient Anglian settlement devoted to farming and fishing at the mouth of the Ribble, had 2 carucates of cultivated land recorded in Domesday. Unmentioned was a pre-Conquest oratory, timber built and ruinous in the time of Ravenkill who ordered a church of stones, dedicated to St. Cuthbert, to be built on a site nearby.

In 1190, Ravenkill's grandson, Richard son of Roger, gave Lytham to the Benedictines of Durham who established a small priory near the site of Lytham Hall for three or four monks and a handful of secular employees. Through faithful stewardship, they effected improvements in the thinly populated estate on the desolate Lancashire coast before the Dissolution. Supreme arbiters in all matters, they drew income from tithes, rents, mortuaries, oblations, moorages, grinding of corn, use of the common oven, fines of court and "le wracke" of the sea. By 1443 they were independent of Durham, prospering until Henry VIII seized the monastic houses and turned the monks loose. Thomas Dannett leased Lytham which Sir Thomas Holcroft acquired and later the Molyneux family of Sefton. Ellen Rogerly and her husband George took over, Ellen being the aunt of Cuthbert Clifton of Westby who, in 1606, purchased the entire Manor, including church, farms, houses and manorial rights, for the sum of £4,300. So commenced the benevolent Clifton influence which survived unbroken until 1963 when Harry Talbot de Vere Clifton sold to the Guardian Assurance Company. He died aged 72 in 1979, having absented himself from Lytham for years.

The sandgrown natives, a tenacious breed who worked land or water with equal dexterity, deferred to their Lord in all matters, depending upon him for accommodation and often for means of survival. Their small misdemeanours appear in Court Leet records reaching back to 1504. Names appear which can be found in the district today.

Two hundred years ago Lytham, according to an eye witness, looked as backward as an Indian village. Ravenkill's 12th century church with its ancient oak pews and pulpit on the south wall was decayed sufficiently to alarm all who attended. The porch leaned, the roof

LYTHAM, the second St. Cuthbert's Church 1770–1834.

LYTHAM c. 1830.

LYTHAM WINDMILL (erected 1805), in the 1850's from an engraving showing St. Peter's R.C. Church (right), 1839, and the old lifeboat house erected 1851 by Col. John Talbot Clifton on site of an old brick kiln.

LYTHAM'S ORIGINAL RAILWAY STATION was constructed at the terminus of the Preston & Wyre Railway when a 5-mile branch line from Bradkirk linked Lytham with Kirkham and Preston. The opening took place on 16th February 1846 amid joyful celebrations at stations en route with bands playing, church bells ringing, flags fluttering and hostelries doing a roaring trade. The Company later took over and amalgamated with the little Blackpool–Lytham Railway, doubled the tracks and turned the Station Road terminus into a Goods Station. In 1965 it was demolished to make way for the new Fire Station.

LYTHAM, THE CUSTOM HOUSE (nothing to do with Customs and Excise) was erected at the end of the Green – now Land Registry site – in 1850, on a gravel stanner, for the collection of harbour dues in connection with the mud dock, and from vessels lying at anchor. Captain Robert Whalley was paid £25 p.a., to row out to collect the Squire's fees. Lytham Dock, properly laid out by 1842, gradually declined as Preston Port developed, and ceased to function commercially c. 1885 when Hugh B. Scott, a local artist, turned the Custom House into a studio, planting poplars, pines and vegetables in the surrounding half-acre plot. He died early in the last war when Sea Cadets made it their H.Q.

LYTHAM 1965. The end of the line for the old Preston & Wyre carriage station, showing the method of construction. Twelve timber arches made of segments so cunningly bolted together that they resembled solid pieces of timber, towered over a covered area 140 ft. long x 53 ft. wide. The railway, arriving in 1846, immensely boosted Lytham's popularity and fame and mounting numbers of visitors resulted in rapid progress and improvement.

LYTHAM SHIPYARD, Dock Road, once employed 400 men and designed and constructed over 1,000 mainly shallow draught vessels between 1890 and 1955 when silting became a problem. African river craft produced here are still operating. One vessel, "Lugard", featured in the Bogart-Hepburn film "African Queen". Workmen and others await another launching.

sagged and walls were three feet out of true. A Church Brief of 1763 authorised a nationwide collection to assist with the rebuilding undertaken, a year or two later, at a cost of nearly £1,400. The population being static, the second St. Cuthbert's was scarcely larger than the original which had served for perhaps 600 years; but a revolution was about to alter Lytham in every aspect. Sea-bathing for health had caught on. The first visitors arrived in the 1770's. Hotels were established, new villas appeared along the front, and the well-to-do settled, having taken a fancy to the place. Within 60 years of its opening, the second whitewashed St. Cuthbert's Church had to be replaced by the present commodious structure in 1834. Five years later the Catholics erected St. Peter's Church. The 1840's witnessed spectacular progress – a branch of the Preston & Wyre Railway Company and a Wesleyan Chapel in Bath Street, both opened in 1846, followed by the Market House in 1848.

Around 1850 Lytham had a lifeboat and Club Day had become an annual event. The Lytham Improvement Act of 1847 had accomplished much and for many years, early last century, the population was almost double that of Blackpool.

LYTHAM. St. John's Church, erected on East Beach in 1848/9, was created a separate parish in 1870 at which time the Vicarage seen here (and replaced post-war with a modern dwelling) was described as "a handsome villa residence". The cobbles on the original frontage were particularly attractive and in the tradition of walls, footpaths and properties in Lytham.

LYTHAM, Shell Hill cottages, at Saltcotes, where salt was extracted from sea water as late as the 1820's, photographed in the late 1920's. Demolished in the 1960's for road widening. Site of modern bungalow.

LYTHAM, an old cottage across the lane from Shell Hill Cottages. Site of modern property.

THE GAS TRAM:
The very first gas tram supplied to the Blackpool, St. Annes and Lytham Tramways Co. Ltd. The extension to Lytham was opened in 1897.   Frank Dean

THE ELECTRIC TRAM:
Electric tram No. 6 at Squires Gate Depot in 1924.
                              Frank Dean

THE "TOASTRACK" TRAM: suitable only for summer use, in the days before traffic lights in the 1920's. Note the fashionable low-slung perambulator. Behind stands the Imperial Hydro–later Majestic Hotel–which had shale tennis courts on the site of the Bounty.   Frank Dean

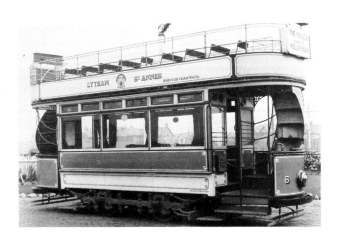

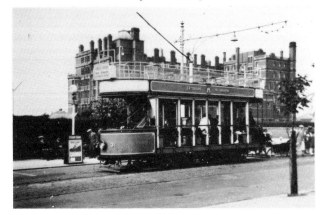

ST. ANNES – Cottages of Lighthouse-keeper and Gamekeeper in the sand-dunes before St. Annes was founded. Sketch by John Green.

St. Annes-on-the-Sea, by contrast, sprang up almost overnight, brain-child of a cotton-man, Elijah Hargreaves from the Rossendale Valley. While holidaying in Blackpool, he strolled along the deserted beach towards Lytham and, en route, visualised an elegant town rising from a wilderness of sand. After making enquiries, he hurried home to infect his colleagues with enthusiasm for such a project and in 1874 he and seven fellow Directors registered the St. Annes Land and Building Company, undertaking to expend £70,000 on building developments on a square mile plot within years. The first building was the St. Annes Hotel for which the Squire's grandson, 7-year old John Talbot Clifton, laid the foundation stone on 31st March 1875. Contracts were let for houses and workmen's cottages and after difficulties and periods of boom and slump the Company boldly proceeded with the building of a pier, almost obligatory in Victorian times.

By 1879 St. Annes had been provided with a lifeboat. It turned out for the celebrations on 15th June 1885 when the Hon. Fred Stanley (later Lord Derby) opened the narrow pleasure pier. Eighteen months later, on 10th December 1886 "Laura Janet" was lost and her entire crew of 13 along with 14 from Southport's "Eliza Fearnley" while attempting to rescue the crew of the "Mexico" during a ferocious storm in the Ribble estuary, the worst disaster in the history of the R.N.L.I. To Lytham's new lifeboat "Charles Biggs" fell the honours that terrible night which created so many widows and orphans.

The new town of St. Annes which already had a railway and a splendid highway, Clifton Drive, linking Lytham with Blackpool, prospered through golf and numerous private schools which sprang up overnight in one of the healthiest corners of the kingdom. Another cotton man, W. J. Porritt of Helmshore who joined the pioneers, began building the finest properties along the Fylde coast, identified by the combined use of Helmshore stone and yellow brick. Wesleyans were the first nonconformists to establish a Sunday-School Chapel (Drive Methodist) in 1877 and in August of that year the town's first monthly news pamphlet "The Miscellany and Advertiser", price 1d., was published by John Allen, founder of Kilgrimol Boys Day and Boarding School (now District Club, Clifton Drive) in 1875.

The sandgrown-uns were still building cottages like this one at Hardhorn as late as the 1770's of clay, timber, cobbles from the beach and straw. They earned a precarious living from land or sea – often from both! "Powering" for shrimps was hard work for those who could not afford a share in a boat. Some fishermen lived more than a mile inland and, for the sake of economy, walked "bar-fuut" to the shore. Farm labourers worked every hour of daylight with no paid overtime at harvest during the summer months.

CROSS SLACK COTTAGE (on St. Annes Old Links), dating back to the 17th century, and last occupied by Neddy and Granny Fisher, a venerable couple who were popular with the golfers whom Granny supplied with refreshments. They were married in 1860 at St. John's, Blackpool, had many children including "four times twins". Neddy died in 1917. Granny in 1928 aged 88. The cottage furniture, including the marriage bed which was lashed together with ropes, was made out of timbers washed up on the beach. Kiddies climbed a ladder into the two warm chimney corners. They could remember the Lytham Bellman coming round on Saturdays clanging his bell and crying "Once more dark and then Sunday" to remind these distant parishioners to walk to St. Cuthbert's for divine service.

Old Neddy and Granny Fisher at the cottage door, Cross Slack hamlet, now St. Annes Old Links.

Granny Fisher's cottage.

ST. ANNES, Lightburne Avenue—Promenade corner, was the site of the wooden Lytham Lighthouse which replaced an earlier stone structure near the water's edge. The first lighthouse fell in a storm in January 1863 and its successor, perched on a lofty sand-dune further inland, operated continuously from 1st January 1865 until 1890 when a gas lighted buoy replaced the old Nelson buoy. It was a great attraction to visitors and picnic parties who could be set down on request by the train plying between Lytham and Hounds' Hill, Blackpool.

ST. ANNES, CROSS SLACK FARM, backing on to Highbury Road West, was the home of several generations of the Gillett family. The last of them, Bill Gillett (right), died aged 75 in 1963. He was a great raconteur, loved talking about his ancestor Nicholas Gillet who was reputed to be a wrecker and who rebuilt the barn (right) in 1796, which formerly stood to the left of the farmhouse. His initials were carved into the beam in the barn and were often pointed out to the author's W.E.A. Local History students. His brother (left) stands in the open gateway. The property was swiftly demolished and redeveloped after the death of the last tenant. Vandals and the bulldozer made a swift end of the last of the cobble and thatch properties in St. Annes.

ST. ANNES – Twiggy Hill Farm, Highbury Road West, c. 1914, with Mr. and Mrs. Anyon and their daughter Nellie (later Mrs. Threlfall) and Bella the spaniel, given to them by Mrs. V. Clifton of Lytham Hall.

ST. ANNES – this beautiful 17th century Keeper's Cottage at the extremity of the old Lytham Manor, stood at the edge of the Old Links along Division Lane which proceeded from the Moss, through the present airfield, over a bridge constructed when the Blackpool–Lytham single line was put through in 1863, down to the shore; it was condemned for human occupation c. 1930. The water was supplied by two wells, one in the front garden. Mr. Edward Fisher, son of "Granny" and Ned, lived here 1905–20. His wife baked pies and custards for the golfers. Sir Harry Lauder used to visit when appearing in Blackpool. Latterly it became another charming Electricity Sub-Station.

The Lytham and St. Annes Golf Club was founded on 16th March 1886 with a "Golf Room" H.Q., in the St. Annes Hotel and the first tee near the adjoining railway station. As buildings advanced, however, the Club transferred to the present site, adopting the Royal prefix after the 1926 Open Championship. St. Annes Old Links, formed in 1901, then took over part of the abandoned course and artisans were encouraged to join. Fairhaven Golf Club had existed since 1895 on both sides of Clifton Drive near King Edward VII School, extending westwards to the Lake where the Cafe was the original Club-house. After an inundation of the sea, the Club moved in 1921 to the present site within Lytham Hall Park. Green Drive, Lytham, fourth and perhaps bonniest course, was laid out in 1913.

St. Annes Parish Church, after which the town was named, was erected in 1872 as a Chapel of Ease to St. Cuthbert's.

ST. ANNES, CLIFTON DRIVE NORTH c. 1930 showing the effects of a sand-blow which covered the tram tracks and brought transport to a halt. The picture including the Cafe of the old Squires Gate Camp in the "bring what you like" era of small tents and caravans, shows the old whitewashed cottages at the foot of Squire's Gate bridge over the railway. The other shows the chimney (right) of St. Annes Electricity Works, St. David's Road North; the whitewashed cottage of "Granny and Neddy" Fisher on St. Annes Old Links; (centre distance): Division Lane bridge, recently removed: and a caravan of one of the camp patrons (extreme left).

ST. ANNES, EAVES' FARM, CHURCH ROAD (corner of Smithy Lane), receiving attention in its latter days, c. 1930. It was an old cruck cottage with a cladding of brick, here and there, and towards the end its outside walls had to be buttressed and propped up with wooden sleepers.

Ansdell was that wasteland south of Lytham township which attracted the celebrated Liverpool-born artist, Richard Ansdell, R.A. (1815–1885). He loved the glorious sunsets, the dunes and wild acres of starr grass and after spending several holidays here painting local scenes he erected a summer home in a wilderness and named it "Starr Hills" (now Methodist Home for the Aged), and occupied it from 1861–4. At that time, apart from an occasional farm, there was only a close-knit community of local fishermen living in ancient cottages along the Common-side. They fished the Ribble waters from Granny's Bay, an inlet between two stanners (pebble ridges) which forms the basis of Fairhaven Lake.

Fairhaven was a new residential area developed to the west of Ansdell after the Fairhaven Estate Company was incorporated in 1895. Among the great problems they encountered were huge sand-dunes which had to be levelled before building could proceed; but in true pioneering spirit they survived the lean and difficult years, foregoing dividends but gradually turning a rabbit warren into a gracious area.

Well inland of Commonside, a road proceeded through the Hall Park, emerging at the Regent Avenue gates, along Heyhouses Lane, High Dam (Kilnhouse) Lane and across the fields to Marton Moss and Blackpool. At the time of Wm. Yates' Survey (1780–6) along this ancient highway, with its grassy copps and pastures spreading as far as the eye could see, straggled as many cottages and farmsteads as appeared in the most populous portion of Blackpool. Almost without exception, they were low, thatched, whitewashed and mightily picturesque and life within could have changed little since medieval times. The natives who first beheld a motor car chugging through in 1896 had to wait until 1911 for a Fylde Water Board main to be laid through from Ballam. Lighting, for the most part, was still by candles and oil lamps and it was a calamity when "Lamp Oil Joe" failed to turn up with the weekly supplies.

In Heyhouses, as early as 1780, there was an attempt to provide a smattering of education, probably by the tenant of a cottage, "a very poor place" for which, in 1783, he received 12s.0d., covering several years' compensation for turning his meadow into a pupils' playground. For 14 years from 1819, a Miss Cookson was paid £3 per annum for teaching reading, knitting and sewing but in 1833 a properly constructed and regulated school for infants of both sexes was provided at a cost of £150 and superintended by a Mistress. Thirty years later the accommodation was inadequate. By 1864 the Girls' Department had been improved and a Boys' School had been provided at a cost of £190. Squire Clifton donated the freehold of additional land and on Sunday the whitewashed building was used for Divine Service conducted by the curate of St. Cuthbert's, Lytham.

For years, the erratic church-going of the West-enders had concerned the Protestant Lady Eleanor Cecily Clifton whose Catholic husband, "The Colonel" J. T. Clifton, gave the site for a new Chapel of Ease dedicated to St. Anne. His wife paid for the building (1872–3) but tenant farmers were asked to give a day's work with horse and cart bringing

ANSDELL, corner of Gordon Road and Commonside, showing the fishermen's cottages (sites now occupied by modern bungalows), the white gable end of Rossalls' great barn, and the creeper-covered farmhouse, now divided into two and stripped of the ivy, which was built for them in the early 1860's by the Clifton Estate.

ANSDELL, COMMONSIDE, showing two of several fishermen's cottages, low, thatched and hundreds of years old. The projecting cobbles below the roof were embedded into the clay-and-cobble walls so that in times of storm ropes could be held tight to keep the thatch from flying away – as happened regularly along the Fylde coast, particularly when properties faced the sea. For that reason, the earliest examples tended to present their gable ends to the west winds. The lady with the sunshade was Miss Ellen Ball, one of the tenants. The gable end (whitewashed) of Rossalls' barn stood at the junction of Gordon Road and Central Drive. Rossalls' farmhouse (left distance) was covered in ivy early this century.

ANSDELL, WORSLEY ROAD (site now occupied by modern bungalows opposite the High School), two tiny thatched cottages painted fifty years ago by the late Walter Eastwood, an accomplished local artist.

ANSDELL, CENTRAL DRIVE–(left) Mr. Robert Rossall who arrived in the early 1860's with his wife and 2 year old son John, with all their possessions on a flat cart from Carleton to occupy a farmhouse here. The thatch was infested with rats. Mrs. Rossall refused to enter and the Clifton Agent agreed to build a new house. Meantime, for 30 weeks, they lived in rooms in Worsley Road. Their daughter, Ald. Jane Rossall, M.B.E., became a Mayor and Hon Freeman of Lytham St. Annes.
(Right) The commodious new house built for the Rossall family.

ANSDELL, SOUTH HEYS FARM, a rare photograph taken c. 1929. For many years, early this century, it was farmed by the Whiteside family into which Betty Singleton, daughter of Johnny and Martha Singleton of Kilnhouse Farm, St. Annes, married. She was a stickler for cleanliness, kept her two maid-servants, Belle and Maggie (Parkinson) working at full stretch from 5 a.m., until bedtime, looking after a household of 13 including 4 resident manservants and a crippled lady lodger. There were 9 beds to strip every week, summer and winter, mountains of washing and ironing, fires to light, boots to polish and a great collection of oil lamps to clean, trim and replenish. Maggie entered into her Candlemas contract at £14 for the year raised later to £17, with one day off per month and compulsory church attendance.

ANSDELL – Trickett's store and Post Office and the old St. Paul's Mission Church and hall, demolished a decade ago – site now an open grassed space with bus shelter.

ANSDELL, St. Joseph's R.C. Church and cows grazing in the field opposite which became the site for "The Blossoms" pub, built post-war.

HEYHOUSES, the Regent Avenue Gate-keeper's lodge (now the site of a modern house) stood until the 1960's, at the entrance gates, still in existence, which gave access to Lytham Hall Park along a driveway which was used by the general public on country rambles from Lytham into the rural districts of the Manor, or as the route to Blackpool, during the last century. One the first occasion when she was invited to visit Lytham Hall by the late Mrs. Violet Clifton, nee Beauclerk, the author cycled through clouds of midges in an almost spooky quiet between banks of rhododendrons. Stealthy rustlings in the bushes, probably from the native pheasant population, acted as accelerator during these adventures into a private world which took place regularly from 1956, a few months after Mrs. Clifton had resumed residence at the Hall after years in the Convent of the Poor Clares in the grounds of Arundel Castle, where she had assumed the name of Sister Mary Seraphim.

bricks from a croft near the Shovels Inn, Marton Moss. The inducement of a £1 prize was offered for the first load tipped and three farmers sportingly shared the money between them.

The principal counter-attraction, of course, had been the Trawl Boat Inn, Heyhouses, rebuilt c. 1860 to its present proportions, and now converted into two dwellings. Originally it was a whitewashed lane-side alehouse when, in 1822 a Manchester visitor gave it a reputation for "bad ale". Thomas Greaves took over in 1826 and down the decades the Trawl Boat gained a reputation as the liveliest inn in the parish. Day and night, farmers and fisherfolk congregated there "instead o' minding thur wark!", squandering their substance, celebrating the occasional good catch or the sale of a cow for a few pounds. Fights broke out, practical jokes were played and in proportion to the roysterings rents went unpaid and evictions followed.

HEYHOUSES, the Trawlboat Inn at the height of its popularity in the 1870's. Mrs. Mary Houseman, licensee, second from left.

Harvesting on the Mosslands.

HEYHOUSES – everything by toil and sweat, even as late as the 1930's. Mr. Robert Rossall (right) recalls that potatoes were forked up, cleaned, graded – small ones into the round baskets, large into the square ones – bagged up, weighed and loaded on to the merchant's lorry for £2.00 per ton. From the left Dick Williamson, Tom Cunningham, Bill Gillett from Cross Slack and "Liverpool Tom", a 1st world war survivor, who would come over, stop for six months at Rossalls' Farm and as suddenly clear off.

THE TRAWLBOAT, HEYHOUSES, and the late Mr. Bob Scott putting the finishing touches to his corn-dollies at the old pump in the middle of the old cobble yard. The barn (left) and the outbuildings which bordered Northhouses Lane, have disappeared and the yard has become a garden. Bob taught himself the ancient art of dolly-making, sent samples of his work all over the world, and made several appearances on Television demonstrating the pre-Christian craft. The spirit of the corn was supposed to survive in the last sheaf cut from the harvest, which was brought indoors throughout the winter.

HEYHOUSES – tied cottages near the junction of Northhouses Lane and Moss Hall Lane, home for many years of the Richardsons; occupied until late 1940's and demolished for modern bungalows. The first cottage had an open cockloft for sleeping, access by vertical ladder. Polecats were a persistent nuisance, a lifetime ago.

The last licensee was Mrs. Mary Houseman. She took over after her husband James died in 1875. In 1880 Harry Clifton, M.P., son of "The Colonel" and Lady Eleanor Cecily Clifton, died at the age of 35. After remarriage, his young widow, Madeleine, became Lady Drummond and she was always given the credit (or the blame) for the withdrawal of the licence. She happened to be driving in her carriage when an unseemly brawl spilled out of the Trawl Boat. It was mid-day. All decent breadwinners ought to have been hard at work. The lady took action, to the loud lamentations of the tipplers and sighs of relief from their long-suffering spouses.

During the 1950's, the writer was a regular visitor to the Trawl Boat when it was occupied by the Scotts. Mrs. Scott, a comely lady with snowy-white hair, whose son Bob was a dab hand at making corn dollies, showed her the old cheese room upstairs with circles still impregnated into the floorboards. There were doors numbered, still, from the inn-days. Visitors on their rural rambles could still pop in for coffee and refreshments for long enough after the pub closed.

Northhouses, a lane shooting off towards a couple of farms and the low-lying mosslands as monotonous as a Dutch landscape, was a community established more than 500 years ago during the time of Lytham Priory. Here and there in the distance there were round clumps of trees, ordered to be planted by various Squires as coverts. Young pheasants were hatched by broody hens borrowed from tenants and strictly reserved for the big shoots.

HEYHOUSES — Smithy (extreme left) and cottages on corner of Blackpool Road and Smithy Lane which had to be demolished a few years ago due to subsidence. Photograph by Frank Dean in 1960.

HEYHOUSES — looking north from Moss Hall Lane towards Northhouses Farm in the distance — now site of modern property — with Rawcliffes' Farm on the left. The latter still stands, though empty, deteriorating and likely to fall to the bulldozer at some time — for which reason it has been included.

HEYHOUSES — Smithy & wheelwright's shop in Smithy Lane, not marked on Yates' map of 1786. Chris Tattersall, the Isle of Man T.T. ace operated here in the 1930's.

HEYHOUSES LANE c. 1900. Fancy Lodge (left).

HEYHOUSES, "FANCY LODGE" *having its thatch renewed in the early 1930's. By tradition, it was erected as one homestead in 1698 of sea-cobbles, clay, timber and wheatstraw. It was later divided into two cottages where many local worthies were born and grew up happily, clattering about in clogs on flagstone floors which were scrubbed and freshly sanded every week. These picturesque homes were condemned for human habitation in 1939, whereupon the local Electricity Department took the building over and turned it into a sub-station.*

CARTMELLS' FARM, on the east side of Heyhouses Lane in the 1960's, a year or two before demolition. The large windows were modern. The sea-cobbles in the walls are clearly discernible. A slated roof probably replaced the original thatch. The farms along the lane have all disappeared since the war to make way for modern properties.

Many undoubtedly would be snatched, despite the vigilance of the gamekeepers peppered about the estate. Poaching was rife in an era of large families and low wages. Rabbits teemed "in their millions", it was said, in sand-dunes and farmlands alike; they did untold damage to crops and vegetable patches, adding to the hardships. Yet, the poor were threatened with eviction from their homes, and even jail, if they were caught trapping a couple of these furry menaces for the family stewpot. Nevertheless, there were plenty of unrepentant rogues who supplemented their incomes with the aid of a dog and a ferret or two, and who even supplied Blackpool shops on a regular basis.

The furthest farm on the left hand side of the lane was occupied at one time by the Jamesons, Braithwaites, Sandersons, Rossalls, Beesleys and Dr. McKenna. It was demolished after the war for modern development. Across the lane was the tied cruck cottage for the labourer who lived rent-milk-and-potatoes free as part of his contract, a charming olde worlde place with an open cock-loft or sleeping shelf with two beds on it, access by vertical ladder from the housepart. "Owd Jemmy" Richardson, better known as "Borge", lived there for years earlier this century. He worked for Moss Hall Farm, had numerous children, detested pole-cats. When he was lucky enough to catch one he would hang it on the bushes at the front as a deterrent to others of the vile smelling species. An old Heyhouses native once called there during a violent thunderstorm. The cottage had been struck by lightning, a daughter-in-law had been knocked unconscious and the thatch was on fire — another re-fettling job for the man of the house.

CARTMELLS' FARM, HEYHOUSES LANE – the labourer's cottage which stood in the farmyard well back from the road was a dolls'-house sort of place, rented early this century by the Scott family who later went to Fancy Lodge and then the Trawl Boat. The rent in those days was no more than eighteen pence a week. The four principal windows had been enlarged from the original and when the author visited in the 1960's the derelict cottage, part cobbles, part hand-made or machined brick, was occupied by hens.

HEYHOUSES, "PEY BOB'S COTTAGE" (left) and part of Sampson's Farm (right) which stood near the present corner of Singleton Avenue, now site of the block of flats, Heyhouses Court. "Owd Pey Bob" sold parched peas and treacle dabs to the few youngsters who occasionally had a halfpenny to spend. Their normal spending money was paid out once a year on Lytham Club Day – three old pence! "Owd Pey Bob" was somewhat eccentric in that he walked down to the beach to bathe, summer and winter, every day of his life. Most youngsters were brought up until late last century in the belief that bathing was extremely dangerous, washing out the natural oils and leaving the system vulnerable to infections.

HEYHOUSES (behind the present Government buildings), this once thatched and whitewashed cottage of "Owd Jemmy Cakes" who also sold a few halfpenny lucky bags or ha'porths o' parched peys to schoolchildren on their way to the old whitewashed seat of learning a few hundred yards further along the lane. In later years the cottage was cement-faced and the thatch wore an overcoat of metal sheeting. It was demolished in the late 1960's.

HEYHOUSES – the old whitewashed school overlooking the junction of St. Annes Road East and Blackpool Road.

ST. ANNES – West End Farm, meaning west end of old Lytham Manor. Site of bungalow developments, 1960's.

AT THE WEST END. Cross Lane Farm, sometimes called "Noah's Ark", opposite West End Farm on Kilnhouse Lane, St. Annes, now site of St. Alban's R.C. Church.

The property was occupied until after the Hitler war but in the 1960's the whole site, including stables and piggeries, was cleared for modern bungalows. At the rear, it had shared a boundary with Rawcliffes' Farm. The cosy little farmhouse backs on to Moss Hall Lane, turns its full face towards the sea. It is still there, unoccupied for years. Offers to purchase and restore it have been declined by Guardian Royal Exchange and its days, obviously, are numbered – which is why it has been included. The destruction of so many beautiful properties in modern times must serve as a reproach to those who valued immediate profits more than an opportunity to conserve an honourable heritage.

Another lost gem was Fancy Lodge, nestling at the side of Heyhouses Lane when it was known as Lytham Old Road. It had a narrow front garden but plenty of land and an orchard to the rear and from the late 17th century it had sheltered generations of sand-grown-uns. Its roof and dormers were neatly thatched and when the writer showed this photograph to Mr. Edward Swann shortly before his death at almost 94 in November 1983, he recognised himself up on the roof doing the repairs. Fancy Lodge, in any other place, would have been preserved for ever. Its likeness would have stared out of many a calendar and picture postcard and it could have been turned into an attractive folk museum. Behind the idyllic beauty, however, tragedy lay. In 1885, in six weeks from 10th July, death claimed a father, Richard Warbrick (40) and his young family of five girls and a boy aged between 3 and 16. Two were buried on the same day. All came to rest in a communal grave at St. Anne's Churchyard. Years ago, an old lady who had been a child at the time, recalled that they had died of eating tainted pork. The Scott family occupied it for several years before moving to the Trawl Boat. Later it became an Electricity Sub-Station, before nationalisation, but was demolished in the 1940's and replaced with a modern bungalow, "Willow Lodge" which, in turn, came down after a short life to provide the site of a block of Georgian flats.

Marton and the Moss

ST. ANNES – the demolition of Butcher's Farm, Kilnhouse Lane/Blackpool Road corner (site of filling station) in 1960. The gable end was a combination of the original cobble wall of an earlier building and modern brick used to heighten and extend it. The bricks fell without difficulty. The cobble portion defied the bulldozer and at length crashed down in a solid mass. In the distance, the whitewashed Kilnhouse Farm.

ST. ANNES – Mrs. Martha Singleton and Lizzie Benson, the serving woman, in the cobbled yard at the rear of Kilnhouse Farm early this century. Martha died 1909, her husband Johnny, a popular and fun-loving farmer, in the following year. Buried at St. Annes Parish Church. Soon after, the Clifton Estate squared up and considerably enlarged the farmhouse for the new tenant who was having to move out of Layton Hawes Farm, Squires Gate, on account of race track and flying field developments. According to reports, after all, he never came to Kilnhouse but departed for Australia.

Domesday's "Meretun", or settlement beside the mere, with carucates (approximately 720 acres) under cultivation, anciently belonged to the Butler family, descendants of Theobold Walter who came over with the Conqueror. Territorially, it fell within the Manor of Layton: ecclesiastically until 1870 it belonged to Poulton Parish. The Mossfolk, distanced from their place of worship, out of sight and mind of their Vicar and having few decent roads and often impassable mosslands to contend with, became indifferent church attenders except for burials or the urgent christenings of babes.

The Rev. Wm. Thornber, briefly Incumbent of St. John's, Blackpool, writing in 1837, described the area in former times as "little less than a scene of moral destitution" and denounced the then prevailing customs and superstitious practices of the country folk of Marton. Even a lifetime ago, drinking sprees, practical jokes, pagan fancies and begetting "chance childer" were commonplace. The marriage ceremony was considered an optional extra, similar to electing for a white wedding today. Not that promiscuity was unduly rampant. Couples took one another for life, worked hard, reared splendid God-fearing families and were accepted as being virtuously married.

Fortunately in 1873 Marton Moss acquired its first School-Church preceded by the Methodists and, before them, by Dissenters who followed the Rev. Benjamin Ingham. They had established a precarious toe-hold in Little Marton through an old local family, the Fishers, who lived at "The Old Homestead", probably of late 17th century vintage. It was thatched, whitewashed, built of clay and cobbles and had a large clay-built shippon and barn adjoining until about 1905. It stood at the lane-side (site now part of front garden and footpath in front of a modern bungalow called "Otter Bank") and was a cosy low-ceilinged place with a canopy firehood resting on an oak beam, a hook for rushlights and a primitive fireguard in the form of an iron bar upon which a new ring was slotted for each child born into the family. In the last generation but one of the Fishers, Nicholas married Harriet Brown on 8th January 1859. She was the daughter of Wm. Brown, coachman to John Hornby Esq., of Raikes Hall, Blackpool; had been born on Christmas Day twenty years earlier. She survived all but two of her thirteen youngsters and lived to be ninety, a fine old character in long black skirts and a frilly mob cap.

It must have been around 1760 when the Fishers first welcomed the Inghamites and allowed their cottage to be used for preaching. When the news broke, the Vicar of Poulton fell into a passion, threatening the preachers with prosecution for this intrusion of his parish. Without more ado, Robert Fisher trudged twenty miles to Preston, appeared before Quarter Sessions and returned on 8th October 1762 triumphantly brandishing a document which licensed his home for preaching. With easy minds, thereafter, converts met and took the Sacrament at "The Old Homestead" and in fine weather a pulpit chair, dated 1716, of redwood and oak was placed outside for the preacher to address a crowd assembled in the lane. This historic piece of furniture was transferred when the Inghamites stopped coming, to the Congregational Church at Elswick to which Nonformist centre the faithful were prepared to trudge many miles to attend services. Nevertheless, the licence still applied and the Old Homestead was used periodically by Independents for Divine Service.

Methodists from Preston were unsuccessful when first they tried to open up the Fylde area in the 1780's. Their Bolton-born successor, Moses Holden, had better luck thirty years later. Having preached at Little Marton in January 1811, he formed a Society of seven

LITTLE MARTON, THE OLD HOMESTEAD, CLIFTON ROAD, *licensed for preaching 1762, exterior and interior. Note single hand clock by Lomas of "Poolton".*

MARTON MOSS, *the Blowing Sands Smithy (down Squires Gate Lane, near the Commonedge) where, for many years, Tom "Abey" – Thomas Cardwell, son of Abraham Cardwell – was the blacksmith and wheelwright. The white gateposts belonged to the first of two cottages built out of the materials from the demolished Wesleyan Chapel, 1847–1872. Nicholas Cardwell, clogger, occupied one, conducted his business in an upstairs bedroom, asked his young "while you wait" customers to sit in stockinged feet on the stair-steps while he fitted new irons.*

members and from such modest beginnings the Methodist movement survived through cottage meetings regularly held in the Blowing Sands home of the Hall family, prominent market gardeners on the Moss. Mounted preachers came from Preston or Garstang. Quarterly Love Feasts were conducted by Preacher Richardson of Newton-with-Scales who footslogged the seventeen miles, there and back.

No picture has survived of the first small brick chapel which the Methodists built next to the Blowing Sands smithy and opened in 1847. Farmers from Peel, Mythop and Old Lytham's West End (now part of St. Annes) rolled up in their shandries or came on foot and by the 1870's the building was far too small. In 1872 a larger replacement was opened in Chapel Road. The old place was sold off for £64.8s.0d., and demolished, the bricks being re-used for the building of two semis on the site. In one of them, years later and quite by accident, the slopstone sink was found to be the original date-stone inverted and inscribed on the under-side "Wesleyan Chapel 1847". The valuable relic was instantly removed to a place of honour in the Chapel Road premises (which have since vanished) and can now be seen in the foyer of the Midgeland Road Methodist Church.

Division Lane, until fairly modern times a primitive track linking the Moss-based fishermen with the seashore, was the boundary line between the Manors of Lytham and Layton. There lies the explanation of a mistrust which survived well into this century between the Mossogs and the Sand-grown-uns. Years ago, the writer questioned Bill Gillett, last tenant at Cross Slack Farm, near the St. Annes Old Links, about the origin of the name "Mad Nook". The reply was prompt and unpremeditated. "There was a great battle fought there!", an explanation scarcely credible at the time. Further investigation, however, established that in 1530 and again in 1532 hostilities in the boundary area were serious enough to warrant an official investigation by order of the Chancellor of the Duchy of Lancaster. Arising out of disputes over boundaries, a house was pulled down about the

MARTON MOSS — the second Wesleyan Chapel in Chapel Road, opened in 1872, demolished 1975.

DIVISION LANE, MARTON MOSS — long gone but identified by several elderly Moss natives as "Emma and Will Webster's place". He was saddled with the nickname "Duck", as many of the Websters were, and was referred to as "Double-Yoo Duck" to distinguish him from his many relatives of the name surname.

MARTON MOSS, DIVISION LANE, an old thatched farmhouse and barn close to the lane-side (now site of Keeper's Cottage), with members of the Hesketh family. A portion of the front wall near the upstairs window fell down and was repaired by Ned "Brethert" (Braithwaite) of Folds Farm, with bricks. Sometime after 1929 Mr. Richard Hesketh purchased the farmhouse and 2 acres of land for £275. By 1936 he had demolished the house and replaced it with a red brick bungalow at a cost of £497.5s.0d. He named it "Esk-Lyn" by which name it was known until it was gutted, modernised and renamed "Keeper's Cottage". It is on the Blackpool side of the old Division Lane.

occupier's ears, the Prior's cattle were driven out, his crops were trampled, ditches stopped and the very Cell itself was threatened with destruction. Despite heavily biased evidence from tenants of the respective communities, the case was resolved in favour of Lytham and the Layton folk were bidden to go their ways in peace. The ill-feeling rankled on and was perpetuated down so many generations that few could explain what had caused it in the first place.

During the reign of Henry VIII, the Butler family sold their manorial rights in the Marton area to one John Brown, citizen and Mercer of London who, soon after, disposed of them to Thomas Fleetwood. His descendants retained their hold upon the northern portion of the Fylde coast into last century but Little Marton and the mosslands were purchased at the same time as Lytham by (Sir) Cuthbert Clifton of Westby in 1606. Various Squires of Lytham summoned the Manor Courts and also became involved in the great 18th century reclamation of the Moss by a laboriously contrived network of drains and dykes. Acres

MARTON MOSS – DIVISION LANE, these thatched cottages with short front gardens stood at the edge of a country track overlooking low mosslands which had not effectively been drained – hence the protective wooden railings round the swamp in the foreground. The bearded chap (left) was "Allida" Wilkins. The girls on the wall were neighbours' children. Mrs. Hesketh, in long skirts, and her daughters Belle and Renie, lived in a thatched farmhouse almost next door. The baby on Grandma's knee was little "Aggie" Wilkins, with her brother "Chummy" Wilkins beside her. Ivy was encouraged to grow because sparrows roosted there at night and could easily be netted. They made good pies, while their heads, chicks or eggs from the nest earned a few coppers for the lads who could be bothered to turn them in at specified farms where they were rewarded out of the "Sparrow Tax".

MARTON MOSS – one of its best known characters, "Bonk" Thomas Wade born in Commonside, Ansdell in December 1849, orphaned at 10 when his father, William Wade, a fisherman, was drowned in the Ribble estuary, and taken in by his Great Uncle George Cartmell of the Folds Farm, whose grand-daughter "Lizzie" he married. They moved into the Folds Row, opened a grocery shop in the front parlour and produced a large family. Lizzie died in 1918 and, working hard almost to the end, "Bonk" survived into his 87th year. Here he is at 82, still putting in 12-hour days.

became available for cultivation which previously had been too waterlogged for horse and plough to work. By the same token, good drainage and adequate outfalls diminished Marton Mere, once extensive, deep and teeming with fish. What is left of it can be spotted behind Blackpool Zoo, a fair-sized frogpond, nowadays, popular with anglers and bird-watchers but insignificant in comparison with its former importance.

Despite the proximity of bustling Blackpool, mossland life proceeded almost unchanged for centuries. Motor buses altered all that from the 1920's onwards. Even in Edwardian times, older women rarely ventured beyond the garden gate and one or two aged dames on the Moss had never set eyes on the sea or on the railway. (It began as a single-line service from Lytham to Hounds' Hill – Blackpool Central – in April 1863). They walked everywhere, relied on itinerant hawkers for the necessities of life, used turfs cut by their menfolk as fuel for their fires. From rushlights, they had progressed to paraffin lamps. The Packman called every fortnight, taking orders; what few clothes they had were made up at home by the travelling tailor who boarded with his customers until their orders were completed. Before sewing machines, he would stitch away by hand sitting cross-legged on the kitchen table drawn as closely as possible to the light from tiny cottage windows. Doctors cost money. They were rarely sent for.

MARTON MOSS – THE OLD SCHOOLHOUSE standing well back from the north side of Division Lane was still occupied when photographed by Frank Dean in 1961. It was probably used for schooling a few Moss children from the early 1830's. A Mrs. Butcher was in charge and Lady Eleanor Cecily Clifton kept a close eye on the proceedings. Church services were held here and the school operated until new premises were built in School Road in 1873.

Everything by horse and cart. From showrooms in Lytham Road, South Shore, the hawker's cart came piled up with just about everything but the kitchen sink.

MARTON MOSS — the old Shovels Inn, demolished and replaced, post-war, with the Folds Row cottages and the white farm buildings of Folds Farm (right).

A Dame-School operated on the Moss from the early 1830's and the quaint little cottage still exists standing well back from Division Lane. In 1873 Squire Clifton donated land for a one-room school and schoolhouse still there in School Road. From earliest days, before the first temporary Church of St. Nicholas attached to Holy Trinity, South Shore, was erected in 1936, the school was used for Divine Service. Lady Eleanor Cecily Clifton took a keen interest in schooling on the Moss. She writes to the Clifton Agent —

"I was at Mrs. Butcher's Moss School yesterday. She is having a school tea party next week and will be very grateful for a few evergreens which I told her she should have. Also at the same time send her 5/- from me towards the expenses of the tea fight" . . .

or:

"Come to the Hall on Tuesday at 2.30 and drive me in your pony carriage to the Moss School. I want to see about the work there".

The well meaning autocrat supported every worthy cause and though regularly wintering in the Midland counties was mindful of "my husband's home on the sea shore . . . and those who might be at sea".

MARTON MOSS, FOLDS FARM, where 10-year old orphan, "Bonk" Wade grew up in the home of his Great Uncle George Cartmell. The "gable-end" (left) was added by Wm. Cartmell of the next generation. The decaying remains of this grand old home are still there, used for storage. Many years have passed since Mrs. Annie Braithwaite fried up fish and chips over the fire for the dancers queueing up after a night's dancing in the "lung shippon" at the Folds. She had been born here, moved later to Arnott Farm, Little Marton, but came back after marriage to "Ned Brethert" from the Shovels. She was one of 11, had 11 of her own.

Behind the Folds Row next to the Shovels Inn, Folds Farm was run by George Cartmell around 1860 when young Thomas "Bonk" Wade (10) joined the household. "Bonk's" father, a fisherman, was drowned in the Ribble leaving six orphaned children who were parcelled out among relatives. "Bonk" became a farmer's boy in return for his keep. Old George's son William Cartmell later took over and at twenty one "Bonk married William's daughter Lizzie (19). They rented a Folds Row cottage at £3 a year, lost one or two children, but in time produced "as good as a dozen", Lizzie also running a shop in the front room with £60 provided by her father. She stocked basic commodities such as flour, oatmeal, sugar, lard, candles and sweets, and was "a grand woman", according to her niece Annie who recalled: "Hu hed a bad leg. Hu'd gi' childer tuppence and a few toffees ta goo up an' sweep under t'beds".

Lizzie's sister Grace, "a nice lady with beautiful blue eyes", her grand-daughter remembers, was the daughter of one William Cartmell and the wife of another of the same name. She was a clever pupil at the old Dame-School, stayed on as an uncertificated teacher and became famous for her beautiful sewing and crochet-work, often sitting up until 3 a.m., to complete her orders. She was patronised by the élite of Blackpool and produced many a fancy pair of socks for the Clifton children. Apart from that, she was a splendid midwife constantly in demand among the neighbours, consulted by ladies who called with pony and trap, and engaged by Blackpool's old Doctor Ireland.

Grace lived in the Folds Row where most of the tenants were related. She had eleven children and all went merrily until one night when her husband, Will Cartmell and a pal went fishing off Blackpool. A storm blew up. They were "drowned at sea" as a stone records at Holy Trinity Church. Grace was left to fend and as her family dispersed she was left with her bad leg and a loquacious African grey parrot for company. It had a lurid vocabulary, a habit of hurling nutshells at visitors it did not like, and ended its days with Grace's son James Cartmell (1864–1929), who married the blacksmith's daughter from Kirkham.

Others in the Row, where no doors were ever locked, were the bibulous "Tinman" who made and mended milk kits, pans, kettles, etc., hawked them around Westby and would "sell owt at aw' when he was droonk!"; "Owd Garrett" whose horse Tommy was whitewashed one night by pranksters as it grazed on the old common lands opposite. "Ged away, thee! I want my Tommy!", he snapped at the ghostly white quadruped that kept following as he roamed the field calling for his pet; "Owd Shopper" and his wife "Murry" who fell out over his boozy habits. "Coom in, tha drunken thing!", she would greet him, though sometimes she turned him out and then he would sleep in the barn at Folds Farm; "Owd Stemp", the cobbler and, best known of all, Will Wade, son of "Bonk", who played the fiddle for the local barn dances accompanied on the "squeeze box", sometimes, by Tommy Cardwell from Mad Nook.

In the next generation at Folds Farm, their eleven children included Jack and Will who were among the last to attend the tiny Division Lane Schoolhouse. Their dinners of fat bacon hot-pot, carried in a tin, were warmed up in the teacher's oven and eaten in the great barn alongside. Their sister Annie, born in 1877, attended the new building up School Road, run by Mr. and Mrs. Bogle. The mistress "was a smart wooman in a green dress, tight-fitted and all buttons. She wanted me to stop on as a monitor and infant teacher. I used to take milk and cream every day for her and Master". Gamekeeper Pearson's widow – he was killed on the railway, going after a dog – did their washing and cleaning. It eked out her 10/- a week pension from the Cliftons.

"JOINER JACK" SINGLETON'S COTTAGE adjoining Whinfield, near the Shovels Inn photographed by Frank Dean in 1961 shortly before demolition.

MARGARET AND TOMMY HARRISON, both born in the 1840's, immortalised by the travelling Photo-Grapher before the 1st World War at the back door of Moss Side Hall Farm. They hailed from Marton Moss, lived in a Commonedge Road cottage. Planting starr-grass in the St. Annes sand-dunes was Tommy's occupation until they acquired their farm at Moss Side. Tommy would only be "taken" with his beloved fiddle. Margaret was a splendid midwife. He died c. 1917. Margaret, buried at "The Willows" Kirkham, in 1928.

MARTON MOSS – 2 cottages on Commonedge Road which had to be demolished after a motorist ploughed into the right-hand side and became embedded in part of the living room in 1971. Tommy and Margaret Harrison occupied the cottage (left) in the 1860's, next door to Johnny and Martha Singleton's (right). Martha stocked a few commodities in the front parlour and her first 3 children were born here. Afterwards, she and Johnny moved to Kilnhouse Farm, St. Annes, and the Harrisons took over Moss Side Hall Farm. The two families remained close friends for life.

When Annie was fourteen, the family moved to Arnott Farm whence at twenty one she married Ned "Brethert" (Braithwaite) from the Shovels. Ned was a bricklayer and builder, the kindest and most hospitable of partners. They moved into Folds Row for three or four years before taking over Annie's old birthplace, Folds Farm. Annie, one of eleven, produced eleven of her own and "Ya couldn't move for kids, allus a houseful", she remembered. "Th'lung shippon had a dancing room and about 60 to 80 would turn up" paying 3d. apiece and afterwards queueing up for Annie's 2d. fish and 2d. chips cooked over the fire.

It must have been difficult managing a large family in a cramped farmhouse with stone floors, no hot water, a side-boiler, oil lamps and candles. Eight tiny steps led to a low attic with bedroom windows at floor level. A "parlour end" with two extra bedrooms, was added in the days of Annie's parents. When she was reminded that the buttery was barely 5′6″ high, she laughed and responded: "Aye, bod id's hed soom good meyt in id!" "A rackapelt", was how she described the Squire, John T. Clifton (1868–1928) Lady Eleanor Cecily's grandson, recalling how he came belting through on horseback or in his big racing car. "He used to visit the Moss School with Mrs. Clifton and daughters; went shooting in Square Wood nearby, shot 62 brace that year when 'Chickin' Eaves' was gamekeeper. Jem Copperthwaite of Little Marton was their horse-breeder and he larned Jemmy Fair's lads

152/154, Abbey Road, Squires Gate. Home of the Ball family (right).

and Clifton childer to ride; talked fine, in his way, a real horsey fella, tweedy wi' good leggin's on him – they dudn't fit him, mind ya. He'd hev hed 'em given. They once took a colt to the Shovels and larned it to sup out of a glass!"

It was sheer joy hearing the old Fylde Dialect at its purest and most musical tumbling from old Annie Braithwaite's lips. Words like "lide" (a few), "gleed" (red hot); "lowking" (weeding), "slancing" (stealing something in a furtive manner), "cather" (cradle rocker) and many other inherited from Anglo-Saxon and Norse forebears. Miscarriages, procreation, hard work and laughter were her portion and her kiddies, named alphabetically, were Albert, Bernard, Cyril, Dan, Elizabeth, Fred, George, Hannah, Ida, Jack and Kitty who was killed at ten when she fell off the duckboard of a hawker's cart. "Nobody'd goo short", her son Jack remembers. "Dooant tek onnything frae Mrs. So-and-So, her husband's bin led off for a bit", she would say. She and Ned always raised a few extra ducks and hens "for poor fooalks as hadn't nowt ta ayt" at Christmas. She married at Holy Trinity Church, knew all, and was related to most of the Mossogs, and truly mourned her good man, Ned, who came home from work one day in 1940, collapsed and died at the age of sixty-two. She survived into her 89th year.

To the north of the Shovels had lived her uncle, "Joiner Jack" Singleton, at the old Dun Cottage. He had several grown up daughters and his wife died after the birth of Little Ellen who was suckled by a woman bereft of her own babe, in the Folds Row. "Joiner Jack" walked miles to work in Blackpool, starting at 6 a.m. The night Will Cartmell was drowned, he "saw" it happening, tossed uneasily for hours, rose extra early and arrived to witness the two bodies being dragged ashore up at the north of Blackpool. Some thought "he was a bit wild, like", but after a brief rest after his work he was always ready to help the neighbours "ged their hay in", to knock a cow's tooth out, bleed it for milk fever or administer physic with a cow-horn.

"Dun Cottage", a genuine cruck structure, probably 300 years old, built of timber, clay mixed with straw and cobbles from the beach, measured 29' x 16', outside dimensions and its gable end was almost a yard thick. It survived into the 1960's. It was one of a pair, originally, but its twin was pulled down early in the 1890's and "Whinfield" was built in brick on the site.

The name Commonedge is self-explanatory, the common in this context being that 1800-acre stretch (roughly the South Shore area) from Division Lane to Manchester Square, west of Commonedge Road, Hawes Side Lane, Ansdell Road and Victoria Road. Until 1767 when, by Act of Parliament, it was "inclosed, allotted and divided", it could not be fenced off or built upon but was common to the use of the inhabitants of Layton and Marton for recreation, grazing livestock or cutting turf for fuel. Ancient properties still in existence, and usually whitewashed in that area, must have been erected post 1767 and into that category fell 152–154 Abbey Road, South Shore.

The writer called there early in 1962 and was hospitably received by Miss Annie Ball and her brother Dick who were the last tenants of the right-hand two-up and two-down cottage. The solid walls of sea cobbles were 15″ thick. The rent was 3/- per week. Its twin had been unoccupied for 22 years. Amenities were limited to one cold water tap over a brown slopstone sink, an iron range for cooking, oil lamps and candles for illumination and an iron wash boiler with a fire beneath in the back yard. Latterly, it was protected by a draughty shed. There was no back door. The only entrance/exit opened directly on to the footpath and access to the "clozzit" up the yard was by walking in front of the cottages and through a narrow passage on the left.

This cosy home where time had stood still was where, years earlier, Tom Ball, a Martonian and eldest of twelve, brought his young wife. He began working on the land, worked for Cardwell's brickcroft behind The Shovels for a spell but, when they transferred to Devonshire Road, took to the sea, shrimping off Squires Gate and St. Annes where his boat was moored near the Pier. After it was wrecked in a storm, he went "powering", a hard life. The youngsters were at it for hours at night, picking shrimps by lamplight. From 14, when her Mother died, Annie kept house for the family, with little rest from cooking, baking, black-leading, polishing, washing and ironing. It developed in her a sturdy independence and forthrightness of expression. Men, she dismissed as "bod soft-soapers out for the own ends". Their "deceitful ways" had no charms for Annie who "niver saw a fella as Ah wanted, Ah'd sooner stop wi' my Dad!" Similarly, she disposed of London . . . "bin once and wouldn't goo na moor!" and modern Councillors . . . "a lot o' grab-alls, not like th'owd days". Preston was all-right "fer cheeap tackle"; also, St. Annes . . . "for an out, bod Ah wouldn't live theer!"

Annie's father, a strict parent and a fine upstanding fellow with a shock of white hair, had been the centre of her life. His death, fourteen years earlier at the age of 88, had happened, as he would have wished, at the water's edge while getting a kitful of worms for nightlines. Life for the good-natured Dick and the kind, outspoken Annie, continued unchanged and the writer cannot recall a more fascinating journey back in time. They belonged to a period when children walked miles to school; were obedient to parents; conversed in the old idiom; assumed responsibilities early; enjoyed and treasured for ever recollections of Sunday School treats; and could talk of old thatched cottages nearby that used to share the same pump in the old days. With the passing of this grand couple closed an era; and Progress, for that is what they are pleased to call it, swept their beloved home into oblivion.